HOW TO EDIT VIDEOS THAT PEOPLE WANT TO WATCH

HOW TO EDIT VIDEOS THAT PEOPLE WANT TO WATCH

By Rachel Bastarache Bogan

Published by Renegade Digital Post

Renegade Digital Post
Denver CO 80220
info@renegadedigitalpost.com

First edition 2017.

ISBN-13: 978-0-9989118-1-6 paperback
ISBN-13: 978-0-9989118-0-9 digital ebook

DEDICATION

To my parents,
who taught me
anything is possible,
if you put your mind to it.

To my mentor,
whose simple phrase
"You can do this,"
changed my life.

To my husband,
who believes in me
and encourages me
to follow my dreams.

TABLE OF CONTENTS

TABLE OF CONTENTS

PROLOGUE

I'll never forget the moment when I decided I wanted to be apart of the world of video production.

It happened when I was a kid. I was in the kitchen while my mother was baking bread and I had asked her the question, "How do they make a movie?" As an eight-year old, my assumption was that movies were shot in real-time, events happening in front the camera as they did in real life.

My mother, kneading bread dough, managed to explain that movies were shot in whatever order made the most sense to getting the job done. If they had a lot of scenes in a kitchen, for example, they might just shoot them there all at once. Later, she explained, after all the film was shot, they would edit the footage together in the right order.

This one conversation sparked something in my imagination. Filmmakers were not just storytellers. They could manipulate time and space through this magic called "editing." I was hooked. I began editing professionally in my early 20s and my fascination with my craft and industry hasn't changed.

Chances are, you picked up this book because you too had a moment when you realized that your career would be in video production. While there are thousands of books out there that focus on how to select cameras, how to properly shoot video footage, and how to produce the video, there's little on the theory of editing as it relates to video production outside the world of filmmaking and television. Most filmmaking books offer a few dozen pages on video editing at most.

However I believe that it's the editing that has the power to transform any video from a string of shots into a story worth watching. As a professional editor working with filmmakers and producers across the country, I'm often asked to fix videos that "aren't working." And often the problems lie not in the camera used or in the framing. The issues lie in the edit itself.

Video editing is the potential to wield great power. The power to make people feel something. Every cut, every frame, every effect plays a small part in the larger whole of how the viewer reacts to what they see and hear. Editing is not about using a technique or style just because it "looks cool." Instead, a good editor bases their editing decisions on what emotional response is desired from the audience. Then they push with every cut to drive that emotion home. Making the viewer feel something is the power and sign of a good editor. That is what you're trying accomplish with every video you produce.

Video editing is the potential to wield great power.

It doesn't matter if you're creating a YouTube web series or you're producing a set of videos to educate the public on a corporation's efforts in the community. Solid editing is good storytelling. Yet too much of what's out there for "how to edit" books is written from the perspective of cutting for film or television. For the many professionals who work in the realm of producing videos for business, for nonprofits, for schools and for events, learning how Hollywood cuts is irrelevant. And yet our audiences deserve and desire just as good storytelling and editing.

In this short book I will give you the video editing tools to keep your audiences watching and coming back for more. For the past decade I have used these tools in my career as an editor to tell powerful and effective stories. I know the techniques and theory in this book work because they been proven through time and experience. My goal for you reading this book is that your edits are better and your stories better told.

Happy Editing!

Rachel Bastarache Bogan
Video Editor + Owner
Renegade Digital Post
www.renegadedigitalpost.com

Connect with me at Renegade Digital Post online:
Twitter: www.twitter.com/renegadepost
Facebook: www.facebook.com/renegadedigitalpost
Instagram: www.instagram.com/renegadedigitalpost

ACT ONE

THE TYPES OF CUTS AND HOW TO USE THEM

Editing is the art of marrying one clip of footage together with another. It's similar to cutting strips out of different pieces of construction paper and then taping them back together in a different order with sticky tape.

As editors, we have two basic options when it comes to marrying two clips together. The hard cut and a transition. It doesn't matter which editing NLE you use. All of them, from Windows Movie Maker to Avid, can create a hard cut or a transition.

HARD CUTS

A hard cut is when two different clips are married together, no transition, no flashframe, just clip next to clip. This forms a single moment between them. This instant, the two frames dissimilar and yet full of meaning, combine in the mind and move us along in the story. This type of edit is known as a hard cut. And when it's done right, it's not even noticeable. Done wrong and your audience runs from the screen, wondering who messed with their eyeballs.

Mastering a hard cut and using it effectively is what separates assemblers from artisans. The reason is that when a hard cut is done correctly, it is invisible. Nothing in the hard cut distracts the viewer or pulls them out of the moment.

But why is a hard cut so powerful? And how do we go about mastering this invisible cut?

First off, what's does a hard cut mimic? Award-winning editor Walter Murch describes hards cuts as "eye blinks." Our eyes take in information 100% of the time we're awake. Every few seconds, our eyes blink. This is partly to our eyes needing moisture. This is not the blink we're looking for. We're looking for something else.

> Mastering a hard cut and using it effectively is what separates assemblers from artisans.

The right kind of blink happens when you transition from looking at your computer screen to the artwork on the wall. If this action isn't accompanied by an instinctual blink, it's accompanied by something else you probably haven't noticed: a blur between your screen and the artwork. Your brain disregards the blur as irrelevant information, and you continue looking at the artwork. This kind of blink mimics the work of the hard cut. But why does either the blink or the blur work--or for that matter, the hard cut? The key is that your eyes naturally keep the focal points of the computer screen and the artwork in the center of your vision.

EYE-TRACE AND FOCAL POINTS

Here's is why this key is important. The eyes in our heads can see everything around us from what's directly in front of us, to our peripheral vision. And our eyes automatically center on what we choose to focus on. But eyes looking at video footage are confined within the square of whatever your footage is playing back in, from your NLE to your television, to your smartphone. Inside these squares, the focal point is not always dead center. It is to the side, moves around... in short, unlike in the real world where your focal point is whatever you choose, focal points in video footage are chosen for you by whomever shot the footage.

So what does this really mean for an editor?

If our eyes in real life naturally keep the focal point the same, regardless of a blur or blink in between, then the secret to mastering the hard cut is to choose focal points that are in similar places from cut to cut. The master editor uses each shot's focal point and it's movement within the shot to direct the viewer's eyes to wherever the focal point will be in the next shot. This masterful use of movement and points is aptly called "eye-trace." Pay attention to every supercut, montage scene, and b-roll and you'll see this very thing in action. Cut to cut, overlay to overlay, and transition to transition.

Utilizing eye-trace in your hard cuts is a powerful tool, and can be used in different ways:

- Keeping eye-trace within the center of the frame allows for faster absorption by your viewer. This technique is particularly useful during a sequence of very quick cuts or action.
- Eye-trace can direct the eye from one place on screen to another before the cut happens. This is useful when a character or object moves around a frame, changing the focal points from one one side to another.
- It can be use to direct the viewer where to look next, even if the focal point hasn't changed to the next shot yet, giving the viewer context to the other objects in the scene and their relationship to other objects.

This last technique is incredibly useful, and is frequently seen during conversations between characters in a movie. Character John is talking to Character Bill. John is sitting on the left side of the frame and looks to the right side as he is talking to Bill. The cut then happens and we see Bill on the right side of the frame, looking to the left to talk to John. The 3rd and 4th seasons of Stargate SG:1 often uses this style of conversational cutting to set rhythm and character hierarchy.

Alternatively, this is also used when you see a character look across the frame at an object, and then we see the object in the next cut in the same area where the character's eyes were looking.

This direction of eye-trace is also used to communicate relationships without words being said. A great example is the famous three-way standoff scene in The Good, The Bad and The Ugly. No words are said in the scene, but eyes looking to another person or a weapon directs the viewer to who in the scene they'll be looking at next. And this use of eye-trace helps us see into the minds of the characters because now we know the relationships involved in the stand-off.

I frequently review other editors and producers work and often when I come across a hard cut that isn't working, it is often due the focal points being in two different places between the two clips. First the focal point is in one place, then suddenly it's in another. There is either no movement to direct the eye to the new location, or the new location doesn't land in exactly the same place as either the old focal point, or to where the eye-trace said it was supposed to be.

The solution is to realign these these focal points to each other, either with new footage, moving the in or out point of a shot to help it line up, or doing some fancy manipulation of the frame size on your footage. These can vastly improve the landing from each focal point. And this improves both the look and the power of your hard cut. In effect, it becomes invisible.

Mastering eye-trace is the key to unlocking the power of the hard cut in your editing. It removes the need for extensive cross-dissolves, flashes, and other transitions to hide an edit point. Your hard cuts can then create a more natural experience for your viewer, putting the power of story back where it should be: in the emotional space of your viewer's mind.

Which brings us to when to use a transition at all:

CROSS-DISSOLVES

Video and film editing is the art of combining two images together, implying meaning, context and continuation of thought. The cut, the moment of change between the two, creates a mental third image. It is in this mental headspace that the moving images transform from a string of cuts into a new whole: a movie.

Cuts can be both hard cuts or take the form of a transition. The most popular--and often overused--transition is the cross-dissolve.

> Mastering eye-trace is the key to unlocking the power of the hard cut in your editing.

We are very familiar with cross-dissolves. They fade the first image into the other, meshing the two in-between before revealing the new shot completely. It is a cut that implies the passage of time and makes us feel it's passage without taking time. This makes the cross-dissolve a valuable and unique tool in the editor's cutting toolbox. It is this transition's greatest power--and it's greatest weakness.

Properly used, a cross-dissolve transition moves the viewer along in the amount of time that has passed between the two shots. It can indicate the passage of a few moments, a few weeks, even a few years, depending on the duration and surrounding context of the two shots. By giving the viewer a few more lingering moments, we say as editors that the previous shot is something to linger over, to savor, to remember. This is something the hard cut can't do.

Hard cuts in comparison, instantly transport us from one place to the other. As film editor Walter Murch describes, it is just like the blink of your eye, moving from one object to another. We don't notice an eye blink. It is completely natural. Likewise, a good hard cut is something we don't notice either.

So why do many editors rely primarily on the cross-dissolve when building video edits?

Cross-dissolves look and feel like they must not be noticeable because of how we initially perceive the flow of one image to another. We have time to adjust from one shot to the other. The two images pleasingly blend together, with no jarring effects. As a result, each cross-dissolve moves the viewer forward, slowly and methodically. It prevents jump cuts, covers awkward edits, and appears to be seamless. In fact, a cross-dissolve used this way is a cover-up for a bad hard cut.

Most transitions, but the cross-dissolve especially, indicate a passage of time between the preceding shot and the one that follows. We may not know how much time, but we feel as though some sort of time has passed in between each shot. This one fact alone can make a minute-long video feel much longer than it actually is. Why? Because of where the cross-dissolve happens in life: when we're nodding off to sleep. It is our transition from consciousness to the passage of time where we're unaware.

When every cut is a cross-dissolve, we suddenly become aware of the edit, aware of the mechanics moving our brains through the story, and we start to reject what we're seeing on a subconscious level. Boredom sets in, and soon the beauty of the images is lost on us. It doesn't matter how gorgeous the next shot is. The emotional space unintentionally gives us no reason to lose ourselves in the story. Instead, we're given to lose interest.

Improperly used cross-dissolves indicate an editor unsure of his or her shot selections and where they marry together. Used frequently, cross-dissolves also communicate an inexperienced editor, unable to cohesively tie the imagery together and force the mind to make those new connections about what it's seeing. Whole videos comprised of shot after shot transitioning with cross-dissolves reveal a lack of fundamental knowledge of what makes a good cut work. The results are weak videos, lacking emotional impact and having no ability to hold a viewer's interest.

This is not to say we can't ever use cross-dissolves as editors. But they are a specific tool with a specific purpose. Just as you would not use a nail for every application when building a house, we should not rely on one kind of transition when building our video edits. Especially when there are so many other powerful tools in our editing tool belts.

OTHER TRANSITIONS

There are other transitions we can use as editors. Some, like the fade from black or fade to black, are often used to open or close a video. There are blooms, which are similar to cross-dissolves except for an additional light leak. There are wipes, which transition the clip from one to the other as if wiping dirt off a piece of glass. And there are the quirky odd ones like spinning cubes, swishes, clock-wipes, ripples...

Transitions, by their flashy nature, call attention to themselves. In most video editing, we want our work to be invisible. Using transitions then become a matter of purpose, calling the audience to notice the change between frames. For this reason, flashy transitions work best when concluding a thought or sequence in your video.

> We don't notice an eye blink. It is completely natural. Likewise, a good hard cut is something we don't notice either.

A good example of this kind used of transitions is in the Star Wars films. Wipes are frequently used to signify to the audience that the point of view and location in the story is changing. Moving from planet to planet, or from good guy to bad guy, results in a special transition.

Within smaller videos, it is possible to use fades to black, blooms, fades to white, etc to signify similar changes in a story or characters development. A good editor uses these tools as a form of visual punctuation and moves the story along. Remember, transitions, whether cross-dissolves or some other creative type, are indicating a passage of time. Use this purposefully and to your advantage.

CRAFTING EFFECTIVE B-ROLL

Now that we know what cuts we can make, it's time to

talk about the actual image in the footage and how it relates to what we hear. Most of what we cut involves both an visual and an audio track. Getting both of these elements to jive together is critical to effective storytelling.

As editors, we have two different types of footage to craft videos: a-roll and b-roll. A-roll is the primary footage in the video. Often, this is an interview. When we're not showing the main subject, we're cutting to b-roll, the secondary footage shot. It is possible to construct a video entirely out of a-roll footage, but constructing a video out of b-roll requires more elements such as narration, music, etc.

B-roll is a primary tool of any editor. It is used to both communicate and reinforce concepts, as well as to hide and cover edits in the a-roll, franken-bites, and other things necessary for the edit but unsightly to see. Combined with music, narration, voice-over, effects, and text graphics, it plays a vital part in conveying mood, information, and emotion to our storytelling. Correctly cut into place, b-roll reinforces our story arcs, both foreshadowing concepts and illustrating information. There are two kinds of b-roll in the editors bin:

- Literal and illustrative b-roll. For example, you're cutting a video about a piece of manufacturing equipment and the narrator is explaining how the conveyor belt moves product from one part of the machine to the other. While this is audio is present, there is a shot of the conveyor belt moving product.
- Conceptual and imaginative b-roll. For example, you're cutting a documentary about a former drug addict and he is talking about his transformation after rehab. While he is speaking about his new life for the future, you cut a shot of him walking towards the

As editors, we have two different types of footage to craft videos: a-roll and b-roll.

camera symbolizing his walking away from his former destructive drug use.

Depending on what kind of video you're cutting, you may rely more heavily on one type of b-roll over the other. An obvious example is a music video, frequently full of conceptual b-roll. A product demo or training video on the other hand will be much more literal.

While many of us may know this instinctively, how do we actually craft b-roll to illustrate what we want? When do we cut away to b-roll and why? And how to we get around the problems when our b-roll isn't related to what our subjects are talking about?

WHEN TO CUT IN B-ROLL

> B-roll reinforces our story arcs, both foreshadowing concepts and illustrating information.

In a perfect world, every shot is scripted and filmed and there's no missing b-roll. In the real world, not so. Even on a scripted film or tv show you might not have every shot you need. And especially when cutting reality tv, documentaries, or short-form promos and corporate work, it's a common problem that the camera operator did not get the right shots to tell the story we want to tell.

There are two reasons to cut away to b-roll: the first is to illustrate a concept with a different shot. The exact moment when to cut depends on the surrounding edits: Is there enough lead time in the previous shot that new cut doesn't happen too soon? Does the introduction of the new footage flow with narrator's words? Does the eye-trace match between the cuts?

For example, let's say you're cutting a video about roasting coffee beans. The coffee roaster is describing his roasting method and he is talking about how to start the roasting process. You then cut to a shot of him pouring beans in the roasting machine. If the prior shot of him describing the roasting process is barely a few words long, then an immediate cut to the beans dumping will feel too short on the front end. And if you cut later in the description when he's talking about the beans coming out of the roaster, it makes no sense to cut to b-roll of dumping beans into the roaster. You need the b-roll to cut to the end of the process, where the roasted beans come out.

But now let's suppose you have a different problem. Your coffee roaster is describing how he roasts beans, but your videographer never shot footage of roaster working at the roasting machine! All you have in your b-roll is shots of the barista brewing coffee. Curse you, videographer! Why U No B-Roll? The barista brewing coffee is related footage, but it's not the literal b-roll we want to use. Instead, the solution is to figure out how use to this other b-roll to illustrate what the roaster is talking about. I call this "alternative but still related b-roll."

"Alternative but still related b-roll" can be used to conceptually illustrate information and feeling. It just needs to be cut together into a different moment in the video. In our coffee roasting example, rather than cut on the words that are describing the roasting process, we need to cut on words that describe the experience of coffee. This is using the b-roll conceptually and imaginatively instead of literally.

When b-roll doesn't completely match up with the voice-over or narration, we also need to be sure our cuts won't cause a disconnect with our viewer. Back to our coffee roaster example: the roaster is describing how his well-timed roasting process brings out the flavor of the coffee bean. We have a great shot of b-roll of our barista pouring coffee into a cup. Our audience won't connect the audio describing the roast time with the shot of pouring the finished product. But they will connect the concept of flavor with the shot of pouring coffee. So rather than making the cut where the roaster is describing the roasting process, we cut when he starts talking about bringing out flavor. If all the other elements in our timeline are right, our audience smell that coffee and taste it in their mind's eye! The b-roll does more than just break up the long shot of the coffee roaster's talking head. It evokes a physical response in your audience. In this case, a coffee craving.

HOW TO HIDE A-ROLL ERRORS WITH B-ROLL

There's a second reason to cut to b-roll: because you need to hide a bad edit, a franken-bite or some other unsightly but necessary element. A bad edit can be caused by any number of issues, either a bad jumpcut, unwanted camera movement at the beginning of a shot, etc. Perhaps you needed to build a sentence out of a few different clips of voice-over. Maybe your on-screen talent decided to brush their nose in an awkward way while giving a kick-ass bit of voice-narration and you need to hide the fingers in their nose. B-roll is a valuable tool for covering these moments, but don't treat it lightly.

The same concepts for cutting when we want to illustrate with b-roll remain the same when cutting away because we need to hide something. Ideally, our b-roll should come on smoothly with the flow of conversation and it should illustrate what's being talked about, either literally or conceptually. Unless the b-roll shot is a long take, it's best not to cut away to b-roll for a single, short shot. Watch and listen to the areas surrounding the bad edit you need to cover. Is there a way to use the b-roll to craft a more powerful moment? Can your b-roll reinforce what your talent, voice-over or narration is talking about? Can the b-roll help reinforce the emotion of the moment? Take the time to craft a full moment rather than just quickly hide an edit point and transform these unsightly areas into invisible and essential

> B-roll can evoke a physical response in your audience!

> B-roll is so much more than a shot we cut away to when we're bored.

story reinforcements.

There's a third element to crafting better b-roll, whether you're illustrating purposefully or hiding an edit. Your b-roll will cut on-screen from your primary camera and frequently there will be more than one shot in your b-roll sequence. To prevent each of these cuts from feeling off, pay attention to eye-trace. Let your cuts center on similar focus points from shot to shot before bringing your b-roll sequence to a close. Doing so will prevent your cutaways from feeling like a surprise to your viewers and instead will feel like a natural flow of thought.

B-roll is so much more than a shot we cut away to when we're bored with what we're looking at on-screen at that moment. And it's more than just a bunch of shots that seem sort of related to what we're listening to. The best edits are the ones we don't notice. Doing everything we can to craft b-roll that feels seamless and flows naturally from concept to concept creates a better experience for our audience, keeping our viewers mesmerized and engaged throughout every second of our videos.

ACT TWO

MUSIC AND SCORING

Music is often the heart and soul of any video. Whether it's something prestigious to convey the importance of the services and products of a corporation, or something silly to highlight the antics of a cat video, music has the power to tell your audience what to FEEL when they watch your video. Sadly, music, like b-roll, is underestimated and under-utilized by new editors.

Now, a confession: I used to make lazy music choices in my editing. For years, I selected one music track for each short video I cut. I let the whole thing play underneath, with no thought to scoring or shaping the music. I made sure it fit the video, yes, but I did nothing to help it. This approach worked, yes. But I wasn't entirely happy with my videos. They lacked any sort of emotional punch. Yet even if I tried using two or more tracks in my cuts, it still felt awkward. I couldn't quite figure out how to make the music work for my edits.

> Unlocking the power of music lies in understanding its real purpose in your videos.

I only unlocked the power of music and how to score it within the last few years. Understanding these concepts have transformed my editing and my power to make my audience feel what I want them to feel.

Music scoring is related to composing, but I promise, you don't have to be a music theory major or an instrument to understand these concepts. You already listen to music on a regular basis through your radio, television and other channels. As a result, much of what you know about music is instinctive, and we will rely on this as we go on.

Unlocking the power of music lies in understanding its real purpose in your videos. Remember, successful video editing is only half of what we see. Mute, then watch Indiana Jones and the Raiders of the Lost Ark and you'll "see" what I mean. The clues that tell us how to comprehend the context of what we see are received by our ears. And many of these clues lie in the particular notes and phrases of the musical scoring.

WHICH INSTRUMENTS?

The first thing to pay attention to is the instruments used in a piece of music. Each instrument in the orchestra portrays emotions. Some instruments, like the violin, are more versatile than say, the oboe. But play an oboe the right way, and it can underscore the uncomfortable, comedic subtext of a seemingly perfect Thanksgiving meal with the in-laws.

The instruments used in a piece helps the audience make assumptions about what they're seeing. Take for example 2005's Mr. and Mrs. Smith. A husband and wife, both undercover spies for opposite organizations, discover the identity of each other and take to a shoot-out. They completely destroy their home in the process.

> Avoid instruments that compete with the mood you want.

Check out the fight scene in the house. At one point, the characters are tip-toeing around the hallways. The music is quiet, with only a light chime and drum rhythm keeping time and pace. But how do we know we shouldn't be terrified of what might happen next? The key instrument in the music is the chime. It's bright, almost like a Christmas jingle bell. If what we were seeing was something frightening, we'd hear shimmering violin strings playing sour notes. Instead, the merry sound of the chime instead indicates mayhem and excitement. We take all this in with our ears and don't even realize we do so.

When selecting music, listen for instruments that help reflect what you want the audience to feel about what they're seeing. Avoid instruments that compete with the mood you want. It can take a little practice to train your ear to recognize which instruments are used for each mood, but it's worth doing so.

TEMPO

Tempo is another emotional indicator. Let's consider the music from the 2013 film Philomena. This movie is a drama about a woman searching for her long-lost son. Played by Judi Dench, the title character has been looking for her son for fifty years. She is curious and hopeful, but also worried and anxious. Does her son remember her? Will she ever find him? Does he love her after all this time? The incredible feeling of longing experienced by the title character is amplified in the score featuring slow and steady piano and string compositions. Had the music in Philomena been arranged any quicker, the film would feel pensive and restless. The title character would seem impatient. And the long-carried pain of the character would appear as bitterness, making it difficult for us to believe her choices at the end of the film.

Music tempo can either rush or hinder an audience through your video. Be sure the tempo matches the mood and emotion you want to bring out with your video edits. If something doesn't feel right, either adjust your music or the pacing of your edits.

DYNAMICS

Another essential element are the dynamics within the

music. Dynamics have to do with how the piece of music rises and falls in intensity. Some music is soft. Some music is loud. Some music has softer parts and louder parts, or it ends with a big finish. Other music has the same level of intensity for the whole piece and it never changes. These are the musical piece's dynamics.

How are dynamics used in video editing? Take a look at the opening scenes of 2009's reboot of Star Trek. The starship is attacked and destroyed by the film's main bad guy. As the ship falls to pieces, the music soars with both a sense of future greatness and of present finality. Why? The captain is going down with the ship, while his newborn son survives in an escape pod. We hear the quiet as the captain rejoices in his son's birth. And then we hear the music crescendo as the captain rams his ship into the attacker. The crescendo tells us that this moment is important, and gives us the emotional thrust to push forward in the film.

Dynamic changes in a piece of music give the us the ability to turn the volume up or down on the emotions our audience feels. Control where the dynamics are in your edit, and you control when the emotional volume changes.

We instinctively hear all these parts when we're listening to music in any setting. We feel the emotions of each piece as we listen. Combined with video, the effect results in our minds applying context to what we're watching, even without us realizing it. As editors, when we want to take our audience on an emotional journey, we can use these different elements of music to our advantage. Use the sounds of instruments that convey the emotions you want. Pay attention to the tempo and use it to keep the tone of the video. Harness the power of dynamics in the music to underscore important moments and reveals.

WHAT IS MUSIC SCORING?

I sat in an editing class in Hollywood, CA. My teacher invited a veteran of the Hollywood editing scene to our class, and he graciously gave his feedback on our final projects. Our assignment was to cut a simple three-minute reality TV-like segment featuring a dog and his owner. My edit already had four music cues, more than I had ever managed to cut together without it sounding "weird". Imagine my surprise when my teacher and the veteran editor both told me my cut could have two more music shifts in the edit.

> Dynamic changes in a piece of music give the us the ability to turn the volume up or down on the emotions our audience feels.

I had no idea how I could get them to possibly fit. The key to more music--and therefore more emotion--in any edit lies in scoring. Music scoring is the process where specific moments of music are placed where you, the editor, want them to fall. Using the elements of instrument, tempo and dynamics, we craft an auditory environment for our audiences to experience.

In Hollywood, scoring a film means writing music specifically for that film. The composer writes the music so that the emotional tools of dynamics and tempo are perfectly crafted to suit that particular moment.

Outside of Hollywood, we're not always so lucky as to work with a composer for our videos. Often we're using canned music, where the composer wrote something that sounded great to him or her, but not in the context of our video. In this instance, scoring involves breaking apart music and placing the elements where we want. This also results in some creative splicing and cutting so the rearrangements sound pleasing. But it can be done with great results.

A good editor doesn't just accept whatever a canned composer gives him or her. Instead, a good editor breaks apart the music as needed and uses its elements to create a dynamic musical space for their video.

HOW TO SCORE YOUR VIDEO

I typically cut my primary footage and b-roll before I start laying in music. I do this for two reasons: one, I want the footage to tell me the mood and emotional space I'm going for, and two, I want a rough idea of how long I need each musical thought to be.

> A good editor doesn't just accept whatever a canned composer gives him or her.

Granted, this is not the only way to cut a video. Some editors prefer to find the music first, then cut back to it. I find this alternative process to be much more time-intensive than I like. I'd rather start by cutting my footage to a rough stage first and then scoring, to save valuable editing time. So if you prefer to work by finding the tracks first, then cutting, this process will still work for you, you'll just need to tweak the order of a few steps.

What follows is my general process for both choosing and editing music. Your process may change depending on your workflow, whether or not you work with another editor or sound designer, or the structure of your particular project. These should be regarded as guidelines and not actual rules.

The first step is to define the emotions you need your audience to feel throughout your edits. Your story arc will help you with this. Does the audience need to feel hope? Joy? Surprise? Satisfaction? Anger? Uncertainty? Try to get an idea of how long these emotional spaces last. This is related to why I like to cut my video together first.

Next, you need to find music pieces that sounds like those emotions. How can you tell what emotion it is? Take an active listening stance: when you close your eyes and listen, what do you feel? Now ask, how well does the music match the emotion that you need?

Also in this step, think outside the start and stop of a piece of music. Just because it might not open with the right feeling doesn't mean you have to discount the whole piece. Sometimes the right emotion will be found in only a small part of the whole. Note the timecode of the useful section, and continue.

Now we move to scoring your edit. Place the music tracks on the timeline according to the emotional space, climaxes, and moods you wish to create. This is the fun part! It's also not an exact science. Play around with when and where the musical moods shift for maximum audience impact. And remember those different tracks you found for each emotion? Experiment and try each of them in the edit. One might work better than another and sometimes you won't know until you hear the piece in context.

To keep my timeline workable and to prevent my tracks from cutting into each other, I'll lay each music track into it's own audio layer. Don't worry about the tracks overlapping as they stack, or not having enough length right now. We'll fix this in the next step. The point here is it to put the musical feelings where you need them to be.

Once the music is in the timeline, it's time to adjust anything that's either too long or too short. We will do this by extending, replicating, and refining the different chunks of music in our timeline. This step might seem complicated and time-consuming, but it is here that we shape together the auditory landscape our audience will experience.

Harness the power of dynamics in the music to underscore important moments and reveals.

The tracks that are "too long" might seem straightforward to fix: just cut off the excess and fade out, right? It depends. Let's say you have this dark and moody track setting the stage of the problem your character faced. Now, you want to transition to the next part of the story where they discover the solution. On cue, you put an uplifting, victorious sounding piece of music to define the new emotional space. But a simple cross-fade won't work audibly here. The musical pieces have two totally different sounds. Somehow, you have to marry the two together in a way that doesn't cause the ear to jolt at the change.

Utilizing a natural ending to the first track is a great way to help smooth this. End the first track by splicing the original ending where you need the piece to end. This requires matching together the rhythm of each section. Trust me, your ear will know when it's right. Once the first track ends naturally, the next piece can start where you need to.

The only issue with this method is when the first track ends with a fade-out instead of a defined ending. Fade outs by definition do not give you a natural ending. But can you fake it?

Yes, I said fake it. Listen through your track again. Is there any point in it where it seems to rise to a finish, only to start up again? We can take this single section and splice it into our end point. It will help the music feel "finished". After the auditory ending, we can do a very short fade-out to hide the remaining notes. To further smooth this transition, I'll sometimes hide it with a cymbal swell.

The cymbal swell can also be used on it's own as an auditory transition. This technique also works with swooshes, swirling synth pads, and certain atmospheric stingers as well. Just be sure that the sound compliments the musical soundscape. Place the center of the audio peak over the cut point of the music track to end the piece and a transition into the next music track.

> The right mix allows for each element to be heard, but without competition or confusion.

Now that the long tracks are where they're supposed to be, what do we do with music clips that are too short? It's a similar process. Each musical piece has patterns within it. Perhaps it's the way the piano progresses through a simple set of chords, or the fact that every second time through the melody, the guitar kicks in. It's these kinds of patterns we're listening for. Listen for sections in the music track that can be copied, lifted out, and spliced back into the track to replicate and create more music.

Cutting and splicing music within the established pattern allows us to adjust the music in a way that sounds natural to the piece. Again, you'll need to match up the rhythm between the splices for it to sound right. But once this is done, your short tracks will fit to length perfectly.

To finish everything off, mix everything together and adjust each individual music track's volume to a harmonious level. Likewise, if you have voice over or someone is speaking, you need to dip the background music and effects to a level where they will not compete with the voice. PBS's Frontline editor, Steve Audette, once called a bad leveling job an "auditory double exposure." You don't want two different sounds, voices, or elements vying for attention in your edit. The right mix allows for each element to be heard, but without competition or confusion. For a first pass, this leveling doesn't need to be too perfect. You want get it to a point where you can start making decisions. A final mix can occur later once all the elements of your video are in place.

After you can hear things decently, sit back and give your video a listen to. Ask yourself, are the emotional spaces right? Are the audio transitions smooth? Are they in the right place? Make adjustments as needed. Just like tweaking your visuals a few frames to get a better eye-trace, make sure your ears are led through the auditory soundscape with ease. Make sure the changes match the feeling of the visuals.

A successful and satisfactory music edit takes time and effort, but the results are well-worth it. And you'll know when you get it right. As you playback your finished edit, notice how you feel and react to what you see and hear. If you "feel it," your audiences will "feel it" too.

ACT THREE

PUTTING IT ALL TOGETHER

Making good cuts and understanding how to use music are two basic areas that can transform your editing. But anyone can make a good hard cut or use music correctly and still make a terrible video. Why? Because there's no understanding of story.

Story is the unifying element in every video. Whether you're cutting a fundraising video for Kickstarter or showcasing the rise and power of a manufacturing conglomerate, every video is told and bound together by story.

Any good story is made up of three parts: beginning, middle, and end. While that might seem like an obvious statement, it is incredible how many videos are missing one or two of these sections.

To be successful, a story must open and invite the audience on a journey. It then must take them on that journey, showing the pitfalls and challenges. After this, it must resolve in some fashion, either happily or unhappily.

While we know this, how do we think about story while we're editing? While I edit, I use Story Frameworks to help me construct and fit elements into a cohesive whole.

Cutting video footage, especially when working on unscripted projects, is often a discovery process. As an editor, you might not have the luxury have been on-set during filming. There's a learning curve to scale of what was shot, when, and why. It means watching minute after minute of clips. All the while, you're building familiarity with the footage and the project.

You must scrub through and listen to multiple takes of a scene. If there are interviews to piece together, the process can be laborious and time-consuming as you listen, and possibly transcribe what was said. And after all that, there is still the process of cutting and crafting statements and b-roll into something that will hold your audience's attention.

For some, this building familiarity process ends up taking valuable time away from assembly. The temptation is to short-change it in favor of spending more time elsewhere in the edit process. As a result, interviews are quickly scrubbed through, sound bites haphazardly thrown together into some sort of a story arc, and then the work begins on b-roll, music and graphics.

> To be successful, a story must open and invite the audience on a journey.

This might seem to make your job quicker as an editor, but it often it results in a poorly constructed story. This leaves sound bites feeling disjointed and a story arc that falls flat. Instead of a video with a lasting impact, it relies on fancy transitions and graphics to keep your audience engaged.

Here's where learning to use story frameworks can help you cut your interviews faster, resulting in more time to listen and absorb what they're actually saying before you start cutting. You end up with a better video and still save time to craft your b-roll and graphics. After a decade of cutting interviews, this is the time saving process I use each and every time.

STORY FRAMEWORKS

So what are story frameworks? Frameworks are a mental way of approaching and simplifying story arcs. They help us see the dramatic arc as a general shape to follow and flesh out. This "framework approach" can help us quickly identify sound bites based on our desired story construct.

For example, a typical framework I use is what I call "Problem, Solution." This framework helps me shape content in a simple story arc by identifying and filling content for three "acts" that look like this:

Act One: Introduce Who > Act Two: Set up Their Problem > Act Three: Show Their Solution

Another way to look at this is as if we're taking the audience on a rollercoaster ride. We take them to a top of big hill (act one), which we push them down to experience the ups and downs of the journey (act two), before we finally finish them off with a gentle coast back to the gate (act three). Every Story Framework has these elements, however where they fall in the story may change depending on which Framework is used.

Other frameworks I regularly use include: "Mono-myth," which is constructed in a manner that takes the audience on a journey alongside a main character. Popular movies like Star Wars and Lord of the Rings use this framework. Another is "Pullback," where I drop my audience immediately into the action of the piece, then pullback to show them how the character got there. This is more tricky to do correctly and needs the right kind of story to begin with, but when it's pulled off right it keeps an audience entertained until the end.

These are a few of the different frameworks I use, depending on which impact I want my story to have, or what material is there to work from. When looking at my project brief, I think about what format might best carry the audience and reveal the story to them. This helps me choose the right framework to work with.

HOW TO USE A STORY FRAMEWORK TO CUT

While listening to my interviews, I find the elements that fit the different acts of the framework. As I listen, I identify sound bites with a marker or a timecode notation, then continue on. Often, the elements are all out of order as the different interviews are filmed. This is normal.

Though I could start throwing everything into a timeline and sort it out later, I discovered that the timeline sorting process actually eats more editing time. Instead, it's better to identify all the pieces and then start cutting and assembly. Sometimes what I think will make a great opening statement gets replaced with something better as I continue to listen and identify sound bites.

This identifying process typically takes a single listen-through of all my interviews. Depending on how many individual takes I have to go through, it can take more than an hour. I'll speed up the process by increasing playback speed, so long as I can still understand what's being said. Once I have listened to everything and identified the pieces, I go back through, looking at my notes and markers. It's now time to start cutting everything together that fit the needs of my framework.

The actual assembly process happens quickly at this point. All the critical decisions of how the information will be presented and laid out are already made. There's certainly some arranging and rearranging that happens based on flow and characters in the piece. But because I'm cutting to the framework, I can make decisions quickly based on whether or not the sound bite strengthens or weakens that particular element of the framework. Every once in awhile I'll need to find a linking element back in the interviews, but the process to find that statement or thought is easier because I already know what type of sentence I'm looking for.

Once I have the rough block of all the interviews woven together into my framework, I start tightening cuts, eliminating extraneous information, and moving on to the other steps of crafting my video.

The process is the same on each video, no matter if I'm using the "Problem, Solution" framework or another. Occasionally which framework I think is best will change based on the material. This is why identification of your sound bites is critical. The content often will dictate which frameworks will work best so rather than start cutting and discovering that a particular framework isn't a good fit, I save time by identifying first, then constructing.

Frameworks are a powerful mental tool that help us both edit faster and construct better stories. They help us see through the confusion and overload of information given to us as editor, and shine a clear path of what to cut and why. And the better we are at identifying which frameworks fit our projects the best, the better our stories are for our audiences.

EDITING AN INTERVIEW

Interviews are used in every human interest, discovery, or documentary edit. Interviews convey a personal connection to the subject matter, and put a face to the emotion and tension of the story. Interviews are not just reserved for newscasts; interviews form the backbone of life-change stories, of creators and their products, of fundraising campaigns, and company passion stories. But as powerful as these stories can be, their impact can be lost when ineffectively cut together.

Interviews are not just reserved for newscasts; interviews form the backbone of life-change stories, of creators and their products, of fundraising campaigns, and company passion stories.

We understand the idea of using Story Frameworks, so now it's time for a bit of practical application. How do we craft a 3-minute video out of 45 minutes of video footage?

There is a process to cutting interviews from raw footage to finished video. This process allows for speed and accuracy, and is something I discovered after years of cutting short, interview-based videos as my primary work as an editor. I still follow this process every time I cut interviews down into rough cuts.

The first step is to get to know your subject, or subjects.

After all, your video might have more than one interview to work with. Chances are high you weren't there when the interview was shot. While someone may prepare a written transcript, you can't fully understand the emotion of the interview subject until you hear the subject talking. Sometimes what seems like a great sound bite on paper ends up being awkward when cut out of context.

This step is critical because each and every person has their own cadence, the particular way they talk and share emotions as they speak. When a sound bite sounds awkward, it's because the sound bite doesn't match the subject's natural speech patterns.

Take some time and listen to the subject speak. Get to know the feeling of their cadence, and let it guide your cuts. You'll find it easier to to break up long paragraphs and sentences when you cut with the subject's cadence, rather than against it. It also helps your subject come across as sincere and knowledgeable.

After we know who it is we're cutting and we understand what they're talking about, we can start assembling sound bites based on which Story Framework will best convey the message. As we lay sound bites into the timeline, think about pacing, breathing room and the overall emotional rollercoaster you want to take your audience on.

Sometimes what seems like a great sound bite on paper ends up being awkward when cut out of context.

You'll want to make each "act" within your video clear. Your audience will naturally want to follow the story because they want to know what happened. Using simple storytelling will guide your audience through to the conclusion, whether the results of it impact only the subject, or thousands of people.

Once a rough assembly is in place and it's now time to boost the feeling of the emotions. Here, we add in music.

When filmmaker Ken Burns discusses the music used in his films, he considers the script the skeleton, the visuals the flesh, and the music the soul. The music indicates to your audience what they should be feeling as they listen to the subject.

We've talked about it all throughout this book: as an editor you have the power to make people laugh or cry. Use this to you advantage! If the subject is talking about the problem, make it feel like it's hopeless. And when the solution is revealed, make it feel as if a thousand angels brought it from heaven. Maybe angels from heaven are a bit too much. Regardless, use music appropriate to the emotion of the clip, the cadence of the speaker, and the cutting style of the interview. Then you will carry your audience's emotions with you through the story.

FRANKEN BITES AND AUDIO CLEAN-UP

There will be times that a key phrase in the interview will have incorrect grammar, or the subject will use the wrong pronoun. Or even more frustrating, you'll find your interview is missing key sentences identifying information or moving the story along. You, the editor, have the power to re-arrange the grammar, and to construct the necessary sentences from other clips and words in the interview. Sometimes this is nicknamed creating a "franken bite" because you're using elements and pieces from multiple parts of an interview. This takes careful listening and timing, as the vocal patterns must match the rest of the edit, but when accomplished, the needed phrase is there and the audience can't tell the difference.

A caveat on this notion of "franken bites." Let me put it this way: I have a t-shirt in my drawer I got at NAB Show in Las Vegas, NV, one year. It says, "Edit Responsibly." As editors playing with sound bites and franken bites, we have the capability of making our subjects say things they never intended. Sometimes making them do so is allowable, such as on a reality TV show. Other times, it is downright unethical. A good instance is in the news. I believe every editor has the responsibility to ensure their work is being as truthful as possible to the original subject. Use your judgement with cutting franken bites.

By the same token, I believe as editors we also have a responsibility to make our subjects look as respectable as possible. As such, we should take the time to clean up extraneous filler words. You know. The ones that sound like this:

"We all, um, try, to like say, well, you know, say things as ah, simply as possible, but, um, sometimes our words, like, get in the way."

If that sentence is a pain to read, remember: it's also a pain to hear. As an editor, it is our job to make sure the subjects of our videos are presented at their best. We don't use ums and ahs while speaking in public. Likewise, we must take care to clean up the ums and ahs of our interview subjects. This also means cutting out extraneous words and tightening up awkward pauses.

This clean up does two things for the finished video: first, it's easier to understand the subject; and second, the subject is more concise about their topic. While it is sometimes not possible to cut out every extraneous word, do your best to craft the words of the subject into polished speech. There is no excuse for not polishing your subject's speech, especially if it's going to be covered by b-roll anyway.

HOW TO HIDE JUMP-CUTS

When cutting together sound bites, and even cutting out extraneous words, jump cuts will result. Depending on the way the footage was shot, or the cutting style for the interview, this might be okay, but frequently it doesn't work at all.

A great solution is to cover those jump cuts with

appropriate b-roll. This can be directly related to the subject, or even abstract, augmenting the emotional space. Layer over enough b-roll to cover all the jump cuts, and suddenly the awkward visuals to your transition cuts or reconstructed sentence are no longer visible.

> As an editor, it is our job to make sure the subjects of our videos are presented at their best.

But what do you do if you were given no b-roll to work with?

After you curse at the heavens for having to clean up after a shoddy videographer, scrub through the footage and look for sections where the subject is not talking. Perhaps he or she is thinking through a question. Maybe they're listening to the interviewer. Maybe they just screwed up an answer and started laughing at themselves. These little snippets frequently exist at the head and tail ends of video clips. Grab the moment, delete the audio, and layer it over the section you're trying to fill. You can get creative with these moments too, using slo-mo to give yourself time to cover a section, or to slowly watch a smile spread while the talking subject underneath the b-roll transitions from a sad moment to a happy one.

Another option for fixing jump cuts is to scale and reframe the video of the next cut, making it look like another camera was shooting. You can use this to highlight a single part of the subject's face, or a hand movement they make. Bear in mind though, this scaling and reframing can be difficult for the audience to follow if not done properly, especially if used in a quick-cut style. Pay close attention to eye-trace, ie, where the eye is focusing from one cut to the next. Keep the focus point in the same place to create an easier transition for the eye.

While I'm on the subject of scaling, here's an important note: in your average, everyday interview-based video, do not flip the video of the subject horizontally (ie, mirroring).

Doing so can trigger an unexpected psychological response.

Let me explain.

I know as an editor you're looking for a different angle to use and you don't have it. But here's why you shouldn't flip your video: flipping the video triggers a psychological response in the audience. When we see the other side of someone's face, it implies we're seeing the other side of their personality. Their "dark side." Our brains know it's the same person, but something is wrong. Flipping the video of a subject can completely undermine the truthfulness of what they're saying, simply because of the subtle unease in the audience's mind.

On the flip side of this--pun intended--this is also a tool that can be used to precisely trigger this response in your audience. Again, the use of mirroring all depends on which emotion you want from your audience.

> Your work will stand out because of the quality of effort you put into it.

Back to cutting your interview and needing another angle of footage: If you've scaled and reframed your footage, it may be that your footage is now fuzzy or pixelated. If it fits the editorial style of your video, try using a visual effect on the footage in addition to reframing. Try making it black and white. Give it digital banding or distortion, or try a vignette. Too many effects can distract, but done correctly, this can be a very effective way of hiding the pixelation caused by digital reframing. This technique is also very useful to highlight a single word or phrase because you've made it visually stand out from the rest.

The final piece is watch the video and refine refine refine. Get the b-roll landing just right. Adjust the music start. Create graphics and titles for your video. Level everything well so it can be heard in multiple environments. This polishing process is what finalizes a video into a complete and new whole. Sometimes you'll have only a couple hours to do it in, and other times you'll have more than a day.

Your work will stand out because of the quality of effort you put into it. Don't skimp on polishing.

EPILOGUE

Video editing is both an art and a science. It relies on elements of psychology, grammar, metaphor, imagery and time to convey a story to our audience. As an editor, you will never know it all. There is always a new technique to try, a new way to approach your storytelling, and new software to learn.

I've been at my craft for a decade and it holds the same fascination for me now as it did when I first started. I'm addicted to the power of holding an audience in full sway. Nothing makes me happier than to see an audience laugh or cry because I know when that happens my edits went beyond just sitting in my NLE. I know then that they made an impact on someone else.

As you continue on this journey of editing, I hope you continue to find it as fascinating and enjoyable as I do.

Happy storytelling!

Rachel Bastarache Bogan
Video Editor + Owner
Renegade Digital Post
www.renegadedigitalpost.com

BONUS FEATURES

SUCCESS STRATEGIES + FIVE TIPS TO FIND MUSIC FAST

As a professional editor running and working at my own company, I developed a few success strategies to help me get through work faster and more accurately. These are things I do every day I edit. Because as much as I love to edit, I also enjoy getting outside and spending time with my family. I'm including these bonus features to help you out too.

SUCCESS STRATEGY ONE: GET ORGANIZED

1. ORGANIZE WHAT YOU HAVE TO DO

Video editing is a process. It's not just as simple as pushing one button and then you're done (don't we wish!). Rather than try to remember all the little steps involved, write out each and every step you need to do to accomplish your video.

> Video editing is a process.

This can include everything from "Import all the footage" to "Export video for YouTube and Upload." Think of every step you need to do. This is incredibly helpful when trying to estimate how much time you'll need too.

The other benefit of doing this is you can plan the order in which you do your work. This can save time since you can build your edit progressively, rather than doing something and then having to undo it later in another part of the process.

2. PREPARE COMPUTER STORAGE SPACE

It's only when you start editing your video that you discover just how many files you have that are related to the video. You've got the video itself, then music clips, then text that needs to be added, logo files and graphics...it adds up quickly. Rather than storing everything on your desktop or helter-skelter across your computer's folders, get organized!

> It's much faster to find what you need when it's categorized first.

On a separate space on your computer hard drive, create a folder for your project. Within that folder, create subfolders for the various items you'll use in your edit. Create one for your Footage, one for your Music, one for your Graphics and Logos. Then organize all your elements into those folders.
It's much faster to find what you need when it's been categorized first.

3. TAKE TIME TO RENAME

Another thing that's helpful is naming your files. How do you know which of your default footage clips is the right one when the name is a bunch of random letters and numbers? Quickly scrubbing through your footage and giving each file it's own descriptive name is helpful later when trying to locate that one great shot you know is buried somewhere.

Some people don't like doing this step because they feel that it wastes time. If I'm editing a video where it's less than three clips that need to be cut together, I'll admit, I don't do it either. But when I'm managing a complex edit with a video with a two-camera shoot for an interview, plus 40 individual clips of b-roll taken over the course of four days, I take the time to label. There's nothing worse than losing your train of thought while endlessly scrolling and scrubbing through clip after clip.

A helpful technique is include your project name in every file name, then include a bit of description of what the file is. This process also makes it easier to archive your project off your computer later when you're finished because you can easily grab everything related to your project.

SUCCESS STRATEGY TWO: BOOST YOUR COMPUTER

1. FREE UP RESOURCES

Every computer has a finite amount of power to use when operating any of our programs. Video-editing software is particularly a big resource drain. Freeing up resources to use is the best way to avoid computer crashes and data loss.

Freeing up resources to use is the best way to avoid computer crashes and data loss.

A great place to start is by cleaning off your desktop. Every single file and shortcut your store there is constantly refreshed in your computer memory. Archiving those files to somewhere on your local drive allows the computer to stop remembering the location, freeing up memory.

Another great thing to do is turn off extra programs you're not using. This would include closing the Facebook window you're not using (because you're editing, right?), turning off background apps like news updates and cloud-syncing, as well as avoiding any software updates while you're editing.

2. FREE UP YOUR HARD DRIVE

Another thing that slows computers down are full hard

drives. While your internal drive on your computer might hold a Terabyte of data, it's best not to completely fill it up. The more full a drive is, the harder and longer it will take your computer to pull data from that drive so you can use it.

> The more full a drive is, the harder and longer it will take your computer to pull data from the drive so you can use it.

Experts recommend keeping your drives no more than ⅓ full for best results. So if your drives are getting too full, either install more hard drive space on your computer, or purchase an external drive to store your files on.

Editing off the external drive is a speed booster too. You need to be sure your hard drive has the fastest connection speed to your computer (USB 3, HDMI, or Lightening Bolt are all fast transfers). Keeping your programs on one hard drive and your footage on the other means your computer is not writing to and reading the same drive at the same time. Instead, the data is flowing from one drive to the other. This allows your computer to use the memory resources more efficiently.

3. AVOID USING YOUR LAPTOP

Your laptop is a great tool. But a great video editor? Likely not. Even if you have the latest and greatest MacBook Pro, you'll still find your system taxes when rendering and exporting out your video. And the more you're stretching your computer's abilities, the more time you'll wait.

In general, desktop computers have more resources. Powerful computer chips, dedicated video cards, and larger internal memory are all great tools to help you crank through the data in your video. This is especially necessary if you're shooting your footage in 4k or higher.

The more data you're processing, the more power you need to get through your footage quickly. If you have both a laptop and a desktop, examine each and see which one has the more powerful chipset, RAM, and system storage. Use the one with the higher numbers.

SUCCESS STRATEGY THREE: SET ASIDE ENOUGH TIME

1. PLAN FOR AT LEAST 15 HOURS TO EDIT

Video editing is a process and it's time-consuming. There are choices you have to make about where to cut, what clips to include, choosing music, making sure everything flows well. Then you have to watch it, refine it, and make more decisions. And then you have to wait for your computer to render and export your video. Again.

> Try to estimate the time each task will take and plan accordingly.

Many people underestimate how much time this process will take. The more complicated your video, the longer it will be. And if you're new to video editing, or learning a new piece of software, it will take even longer.

Giving yourself a large amount of time also gives you a little wiggle room to be creative. You can try something to see if it works, and if it doesn't, you have the time to change it to something else.

Remember that to-do list you made in Success Strategy 1? Here's where it's vital. While some processes can take very little time, for example copying your logo files to your project folders, some tasks can take a while. Even moving footage from your camera to your computer can take a while if there's a lot of it. Try to estimate the time each task will take and plan accordingly.

Personally, I recommend planning at least 15 hours to complete a video, even the simpler ones. This gives you time to do the work, get through problems when they arise, and still feel confident you can make your deadline. Remember, this is just 15 hours to complete the edit. If you're filming and gathering your materials, it can take even longer.

2. PLAN FOR THE RENDER AND EXPORT

Taking short breaks in the process helps your brain rest and get ready for the next round of editing decisions!

The more effects, layers, and graphics your video has, the longer it can take to render and export your final video. If your computer system is built like mine with 32GB of RAM and a 12-Core processor, this time is very minimal. But if you're cutting on a computer with only 4GB of RAM and a dual-core chipset, you will have to wait for your computer to calculate and render your cuts.

While there's no way to be certain how long these processes will take before you start, the more you cut on your computer the more you'll get an idea of how long you'll have to wait for each render and each export. In the past on slower computers, I've waited 20 minutes for a five second clip to render the color and vignette effects I had placed on the clip. And sometimes a 5-minute completed video took 45 minutes to export out.

Having the expectation that these things will take TIME is important to you being able to complete your edit without over-stressing yourself.

And while you're waiting for renders and exports, feel free to go do something else. Taking short breaks in the process helps your brain rest and get ready for the next round of editing decisions!

SUCCESS STRATEGY FOUR: CUT SYSTEMATICALLY

1. DO ONE THING AT A TIME

As previously mentioned in other Success Strategies, video editing is a process. And while it's a creative one, it is possible to approach it with a bit of an "assembly-line" mentality. Doing so allows you to accomplish the edit faster, with minimal undoing and rearranging of your edits as you go.

When some people begin cutting, they'll frequently build out the very beginning of the video, refine it until the beginning is finished and feels "done," and then continue forward with the next section. They'll continue like this until they reach the end.

While this method works and will get your video edited, there frequently are two problems with this: 1), it's time-consuming to edit this way, 2), what happens if a decision you make in the middle of the video changes something in the beginning? You have to go back and undo the beginning.

> Think of your edit like an assembly line and do things from the foundational up to the detail level.

Rather than work like this, think of your edit like an assembly line and do things from the foundational up to the detail level. In my own workflow design, that typically looks like this:

- First cut the video elements of the video
- This includes any interviews and b-roll
- Add in music clips to help define the emotional space.
- Adjust and tweak as necessary
- Then add in sound effects (if using) and any transition effects
- Then add in your graphic elements including logos, text, etc.
- This includes lower-thirds, opening titles, end titles, etc
- Then listen and adjust audio levels as needed so everything can be heard
- Do any color-correction if needed
- Render and export!

2. KEEP DRAFT VERSIONS IN SEPARATE TIMELINES

Most video editing programs allow you to create multiple timelines within one project. Rather than cutting each version of my video within the same timeline, I will often create multiple timelines, one for each version of the edit as I get closer and closer to refining the finished piece. Why?

It often happens that I'll try to adjust something in a later draft, only to want to go back to an idea I had in my first or second draft. If I continued to cut within the original timeline, I lose all that original work and have to figure out how to rebuild it. By keeping multiple timelines, I'm able to track the changes and easily rebuild or adjust my sequences with earlier material without wasting lots of time.

This is also easier that keeping multiple project files for different versions of the video. Just keep everything tidy and in one place for easy access.

FIVE TIPS FOR FINDING MUSIC FAST

Finding the right music is often an editor's bane of existence. It takes so much time to find the right piece! After years of cutting, I've developed my own little system for finding music quickly. If hunting for the right music has you pulling your hair out and wasting time, use my five handy tips for finding that elusive track fast!

> As you're searching for music, listen for those signature moods that help confirm the emotion in your story.

1. DON'T LOOK FOR MUSIC BEFORE YOU START CUTTING

Wait, what? How can one edit if there's no music? Hate to break it to you, but if you're needing your music to inspire your video, then you might want to reconsider why you're making the video to begin with. Unless you're making a music video, your cuts should be inspired by the story you're trying to tell and the footage you're working with.

2. LET YOUR FOOTAGE TELL YOU WHAT YOU NEED

Trying to find music without knowing what your footage is trying to tell you can result with you either forcing your edit to fit your desired music, or, scrapping the music track anyways. By spending time roughly cutting and identifying your story, you can quickly discover the moods your video is going through as the story unfolds.

The more you practice this mood identification, you'll be able to scrub through your footage and note these without having to cut together much. You'll also become better at identifying these moods earlier in the production process when you're handed a script or story concept.

3. SEARCH WITH YOUR MOODS IN MIND

Once you've identified your key moods, now start looking for music. When I do this, I like to imagine that I'm scoring my video as if I were scoring an episode of television. Think of your favorite TV series. The editors will use the same music tracks (or similar music tracks) to highlight the same types of moods throughout the show. This helps the show have a consistent feeling to it. Likewise, as you're searching for music, listen for those signature moods that help confirm the emotion in your story.

> Unless you're making a music video, your cuts should be inspired by the story you're trying to tell and the footage you're working with.

Also, pick two or three different options within each mood type you need. It's not often to nail it in one single track. By pulling in a few options, you'll give yourself more flexibility in your NLE, limiting how often you'll need leave it to search again.

4. START EXPERIMENTING WITH YOUR CUTS

Now that you've got musical options, start playing around with them in your timeline. Did you get the mood right? Does the tempo and musical instruments work with your footage? Do you really need music there? If you've based your edit on your cuts and not your music, you may find that it's possible to let something play quiet. Remember, silence is a mood too.

5. WHEN ALL ELSE FAILS, REDEFINE THE MOOD

> If you've based your edit on your cuts and not your music, you may find that it's possible to let something play quiet.

It is still possible to find that some of your tracks won't fit at all. You'll know it by a feeling when you watch your video. Something about the footage and the music just won't jive. If this is the case, try redefining your mood. It's possible that the emotion you want your audience to feel at this moment can't be conveyed by the current music selection because the mood is wrong.

YOUR FREE GIFT

SOLVE PROBLEMS, BETTER EDITS

Are you an editor or producer often working alone on your projects? Do you ever feel like your cuts aren't working? Do you ever wish you could have another set of eyes on your video and someone to tell you what to fix to make it better?

I offer video-editing review services to my clients across the country. I watch the video, make detailed notes, and then send it back to you so you know EXACTLY what to fix. This service is worth $195, but for you, book reader, this service is available to you for FREE!

Your FREE video review is available at www.renegadedigitalpost.com/stuck-in-your-edit.

You'll get:

- Honest & Professional Feedback
- Experienced Problem-Solving
- Guaranteed Solutions

Everything comes back to you in color-coded notes so you know what works, what things I would fix but are up to you, and what things must be fixed for maximum impact.

Your FREE GIFT is waiting for you at www.renegadedigitalpost.com/stuck-in-your-edit.

ABOUT THE AUTHOR

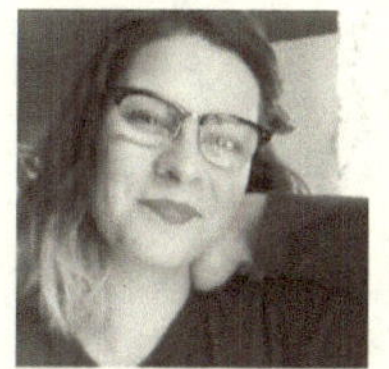

Rachel Bastarache Bogan is a professional editor living in Denver, Colorado. For the past decade she has specialized in providing compelling and creative edits to corporate businesses, nonprofits and individuals. Her post-production company, Renegade Digital Post, partners with filmmakers and producers across the country and assists them with their post-production workflows and processes. She has written about video editing since 2015.

When she's not editing or building her company, you'll often find her traveling and exploring the American Southwest, hiking in the Rockies, or baking gluten-free baked goods.

You can follow her online:

Twitter: www.twitter.com/rachelfinder
Instagram: www.instagram.com/rachelfinder
Web: www.rachelfinder.com

You can follow Renegade Digital Post online:

Twitter: www.twitter.com/renegadepost
Facebook: www.facebook.com/renegadedigitalpost
Instagram: www.instagram.com/renegadedigitalpost
Web: www.renegadedigitalpost.com

BOOK CREDITS

Book Layout: Rachel Bastarache Bogan
Title Text: Oswald and Syncopate,
Google Font Library
Copy Type: Adobe Garamond Pro

Cover Design: Rachel Bastarache Bogan
Cover Photo: Rachel Bastarache Bogan

NOTES

NOTES

NOTES

NOTES

NOTES

NOTES

NOTES

www.ingramcontent.com/pod-product-compliance
Lightning Source LLC
La Vergne TN
LVHW051012080826
845145LV00009B/2590

* 9 7 8 0 9 9 8 9 1 1 8 1 6 *